WUNDERKEYS INT

POP STUDIES FOR PIANO 3

A Pop-Infused Lesson Companion To Reinforce
Scales, Chords, Triads, And Left-Hand Patterns

WunderKeys Intermediate Pop Studies For Piano 3 by Andrea and Trevor Dow
Copyright © 2020 Teach Music Today Learning Solutions
www.teachpianotoday.com and www.wunderkeys.com

WunderKeys Intermediate Pop Studies For Piano 3 is jam-packed with pop-infused piano studies. Get ready for a cool workout in the keys of E Flat Major, C Minor, E Major, C Sharp Minor, A Flat Major, and F Minor as you turn technical exercises into powerful pop music.

TABLE OF CONTENTS

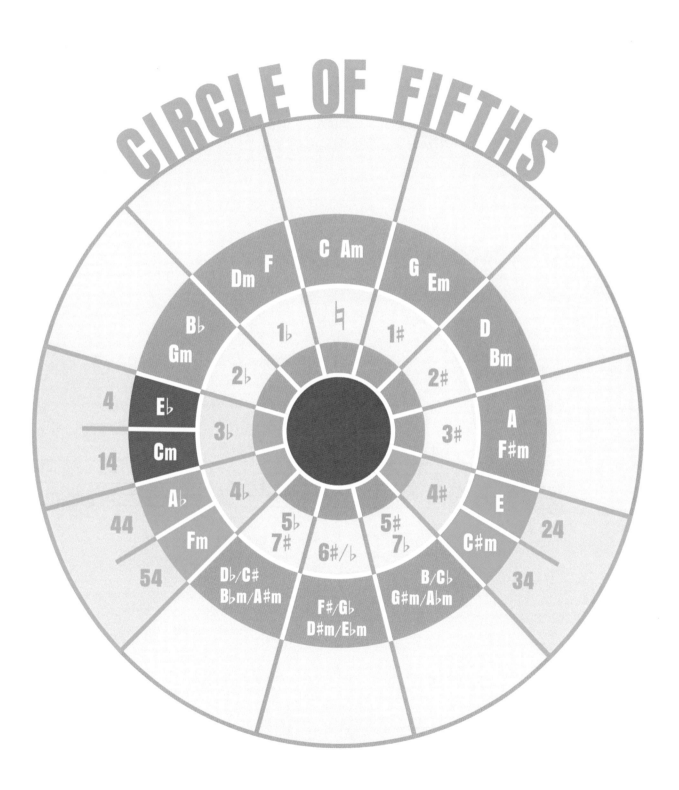

CIRCLE OF FIFTHS

E FLAT MAJOR
E FLAT MAJOR

It's time to power up your piano skills in the key of E flat major with pop-infused scale practice, lead sheet triad training, chord crunching, and left-hand pattern improv. **Let's get started!**

E FLAT MAJOR MAP

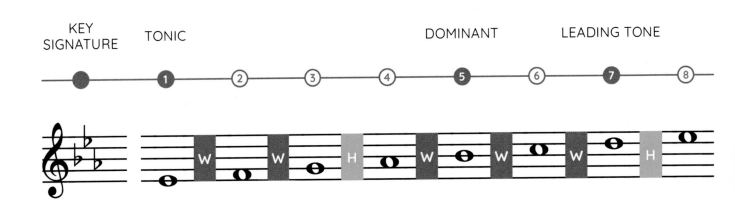

POP PIANO CHORDS

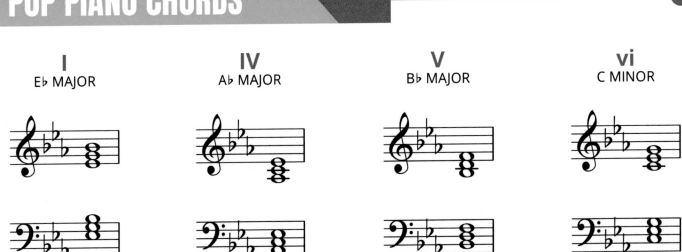

I	IV	V	vi
Eb MAJOR	Ab MAJOR	Bb MAJOR	C MINOR

E FLAT MAJOR SCALE PRACTICE

E FLAT MAJOR SCALE

Practice playing a two-octave E flat major scale using the fingering patterns on the keyboard images and the notes on the grand staff.

LH Pattern

RH Pattern

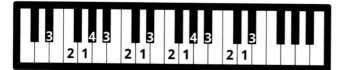

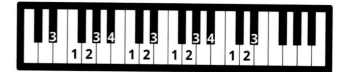

CONTRARY MOTION

Practice playing a two-octave E flat major scale in contrary motion. When you are ready, play the scale-focused pop piano piece on the following page.

ADRIFT
AN E FLAT MAJOR SCALE STUDY

ADRIFT
AN E FLAT MAJOR SCALE STUDY

E FLAT MAJOR
E FLAT MAJOR

Let's put some pop in your triad training with lead sheets. **A lead sheet** uses chord symbols above the treble staff in place of the bass staff. Chord symbols dictate which chords your left hand plays while accompanying your right hand.

LET'S GET STARTED

1 The E flat major triad consists of the I chord (root) and its first and second inversions. Let's practice playing the triad of E flat major. We'll begin with a solid triad.

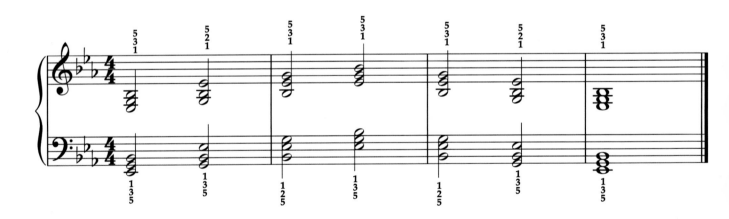

▶ Now let's practice playing the broken triad of E flat major. When playing a broken triad your tone should be smooth and even. Be careful not to accent the first note of each broken inversion.

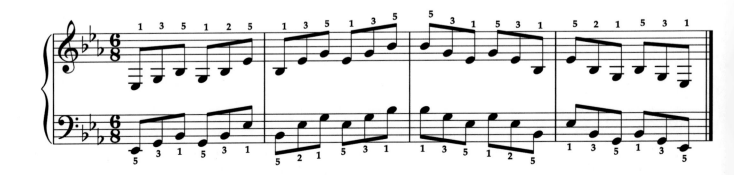

2 Next, let's learn how to play from a lead sheet. When playing from a lead sheet, the chord symbols are performed as held fifths, like this:

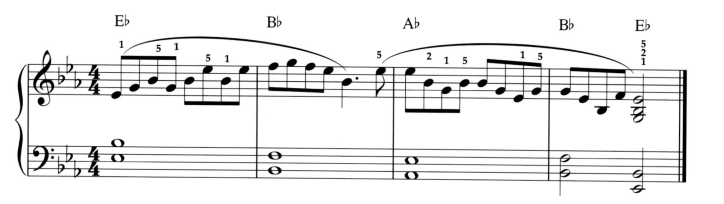

3 Finally, play the lead sheet below to rock the E flat major triad (add pedal when comfortable).

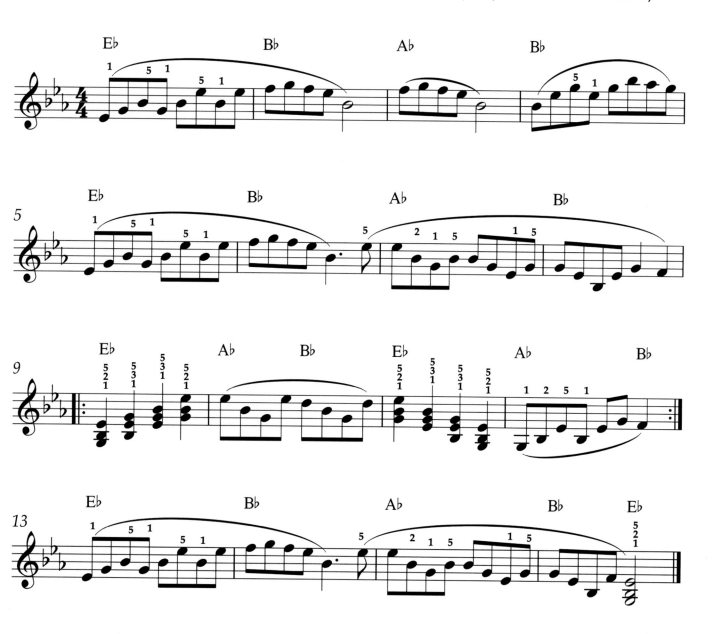

SIGHT READING

Let's explore the primary chords of E flat major. Can you find the I, IV, V, and vi chords below?

Beginning at the red box and ending at the green box, play the four measures of music that rest on the path. Next, I will use a colored crayon to draw a new four-measure path that begins at the red box and ends at the green box. Try playing along the new path. Let's play again.

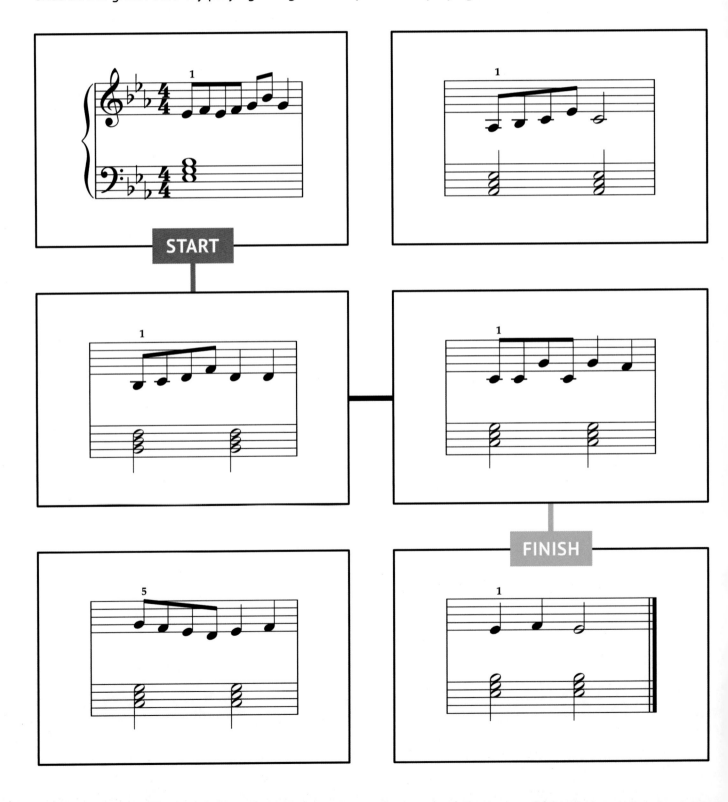

LAP TAP CLAP DUET

Let's reinforce the primary chords of E flat major with a Lap Tap Clap Rhythm Duet.

To begin, practice the body percussion above the grand staff below. Stem-down notes are performed by tapping both hands on your lap. Stem-up notes are performed by clapping your hands together. X note heads are performed by tapping your knuckles on a hard surface. Next, I will play the music as an accompaniment while you perform the body percussion. **Finally, let's switch roles.**

POP IMPROV
LEFT-HAND PATTERNS

Let's create a pop-worthy piano experience with left-hand patterns and improvisation. To begin, practice the left-hand pattern below. Then, when you are ready, show off your improv skills on the piece that follows this page.

LET'S GET STARTED

1 First, practice playing the octave leap pattern on the primary chords below.

Eb (I)   Ab (IV)   Bb (V)   Cm (vi)

2 Using any combination of notes from the E flat major five-finger scale, practice improvising a melody to match the provided rhythm as you play the left-hand chord progression below.

HUMBLE
A POP PATTERN STUDY

Let's try again! As you play this piece, use any combination of notes from the
E flat major five-finger scale to improvise a melody that matches the provided rhythm.

C MINOR
C MINOR

It's time to power up your piano skills in the key of C minor with pop-infused scale practice, lead sheet triad training, chord crunching, and left-hand pattern improv. **Let's get started!**

C MINOR MAP

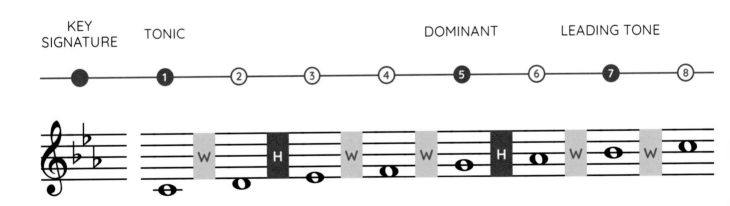

KEY SIGNATURE   TONIC   DOMINANT   LEADING TONE

POP PIANO CHORDS

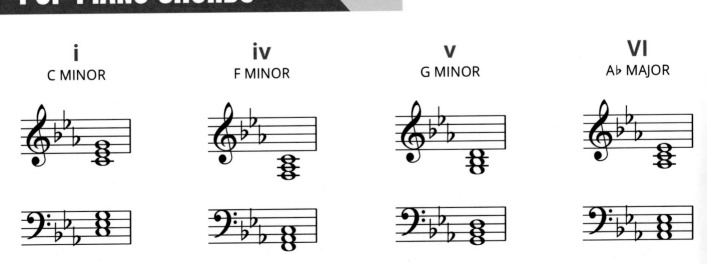

i	**iv**	**v**	**VI**
C MINOR	F MINOR	G MINOR	A♭ MAJOR

C MINOR
SCALE PRACTICE

NATURAL MINOR SCALE

Practice playing a two-octave C natural minor scale using the fingering patterns on the keyboard images and the notes on the grand staff.

LH Pattern

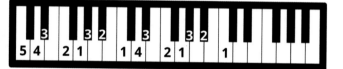

RH Pattern

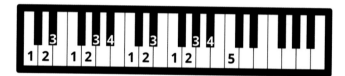

HARMONIC MINOR SCALE

When playing the C harmonic minor scale, the leading tone (7th) is raised a half step. This is indicated by the colored notes on the staff below. Practice playing the scale.

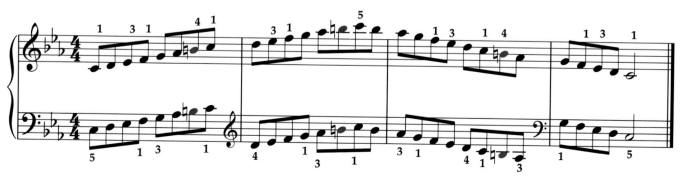

EXHALE
A C MINOR SCALE STUDY

With Intensity

EXHALE
A C MINOR SCALE STUDY

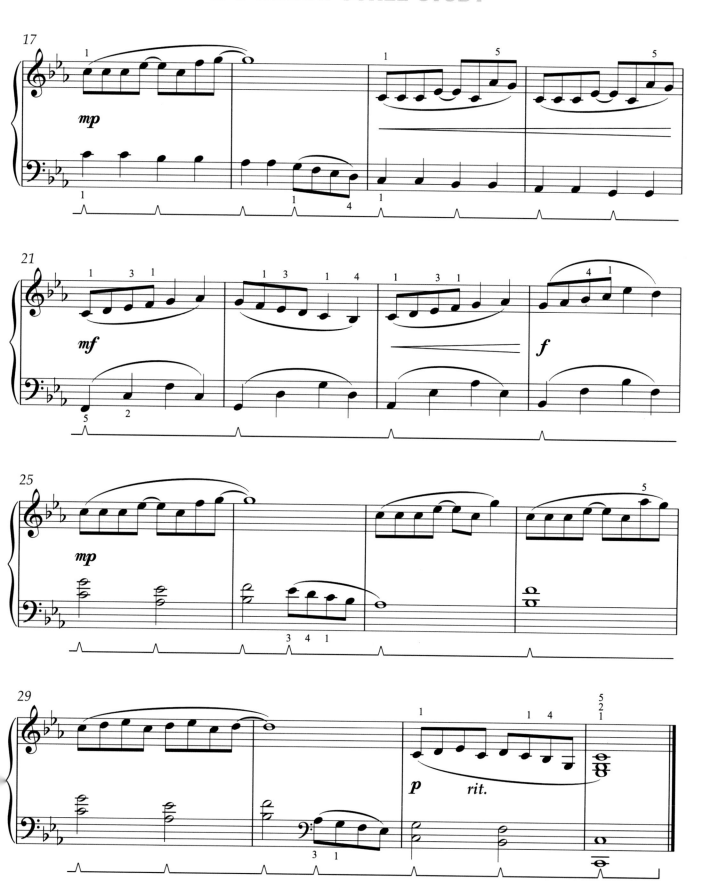

Let's put some pop in your triad training with lead sheets. **A lead sheet** uses chord symbols above the treble staff in place of the bass staff. Chord symbols dictate which chords your left hand plays while accompanying your right hand.

LET'S GET STARTED

1 The C minor triad consists of the i chord (root) and its first and second inversions. Let's practice playing the triad of C minor. We'll begin with a solid triad.

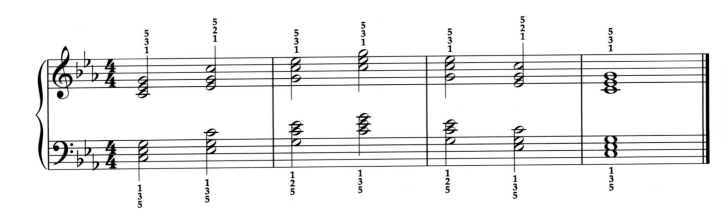

▶ Now let's practice playing the broken triad of C minor. When playing a broken triad your tone should be smooth and even. Be careful not to accent the first note of each broken inversion.

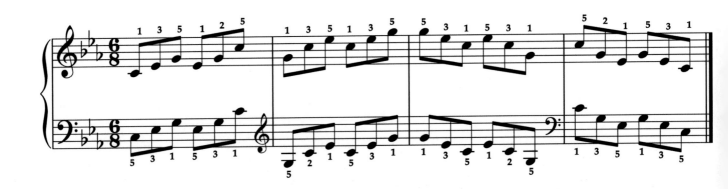

2 Next, let's learn how to play from a lead sheet. When playing from a lead sheet, the chord symbols are performed as held fifths, like this:

3 Finally, play the lead sheet below to rock the C minor triad (add pedal when comfortable).

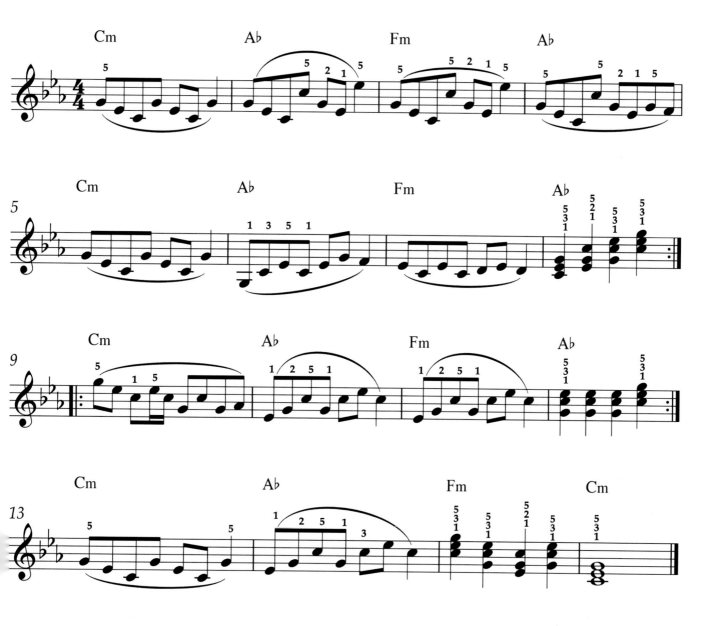

SIGHT READING

Let's explore the primary chords of C minor. Can you find the i, iv, v, and VI chords in the music below?

Beginning at the purple box and ending at the yellow box, play the four measures of music that rest on the path. Next, I will use a colored crayon to draw a new four-measure path that begins at the purple box and ends at the yellow box. Try playing along the new path. Let's play again.

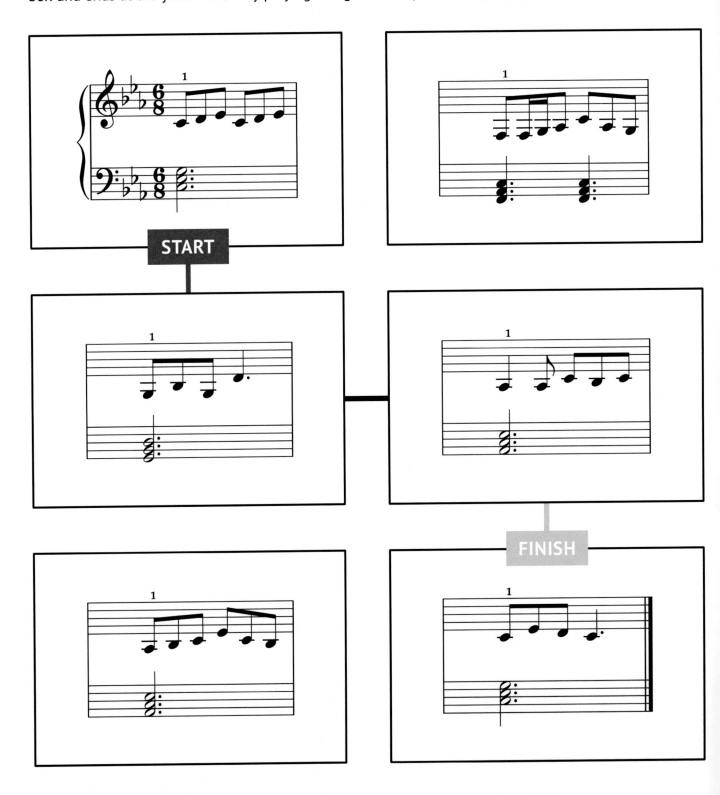

LAP TAP CLAP DUET

Let's reinforce the primary chords of C minor with a Lap Tap Clap Rhythm Duet.

To begin, practice the body percussion above the grand staff below. Stem-down notes are performed by tapping both hands on your lap. Stem-up notes are performed by clapping your hands together. X note heads are performed by tapping your knuckles on a hard surface. Next, I will play the music as an accompaniment while you perform the body percussion. **Finally, let's switch roles.**

POP IMPROV
LEFT-HAND PATTERNS

Let's create a pop-worthy piano experience with left-hand patterns and improvisation. To begin, practice the left-hand pattern below. Then, when you are ready, show off your improv skills on the piece that follows this page.

LET'S GET STARTED

1 First, practice playing the hand-over-hand pattern on the primary chords below.

Cm (i)   **Fm (iv)**   **Gm (v)**   **A♭ (VI)**

2 Using any combination of notes from the C minor five-finger scale, practice improvising a melody to match the provided rhythm as you play the left-hand chord progression below.

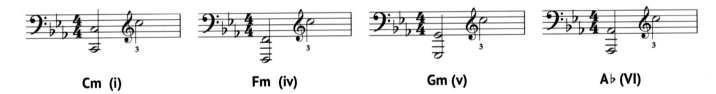

AVALANCHE
A POP PATTERN STUDY

Let's try again! As you play this piece, use any combination of notes from the
C minor five-finger scale to improvise a melody that matches the provided rhythm.

With Fire

E MAJOR
E MAJOR

It's time to power up your piano skills in the key of E major with pop-infused scale practice, lead sheet triad training, chord crunching, and left-hand pattern improv. **Let's get started!**

E MAJOR MAP

KEY SIGNATURE   TONIC   DOMINANT   LEADING TONE

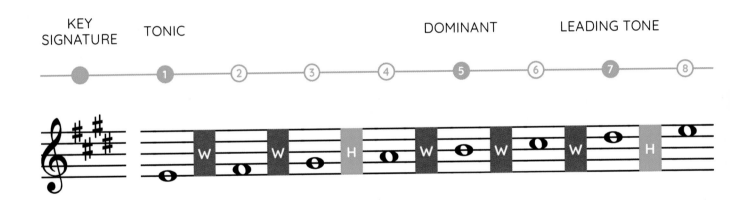

POP PIANO CHORDS

I	IV	V	vi
E MAJOR	A MAJOR	B MAJOR	C# MINOR

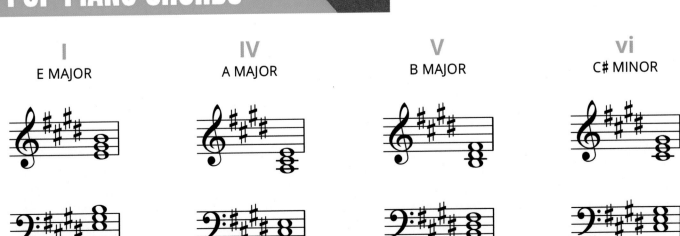

E MAJOR SCALE PRACTICE

E MAJOR SCALE

Practice playing a two-octave E major scale using the fingering patterns on the keyboard images and the notes on the grand staff.

LH Pattern

RH Pattern

CONTRARY MOTION

Practice playing a two-octave E major scale in contrary motion. When you are ready, play the scale-focused pop piano piece on the following page.

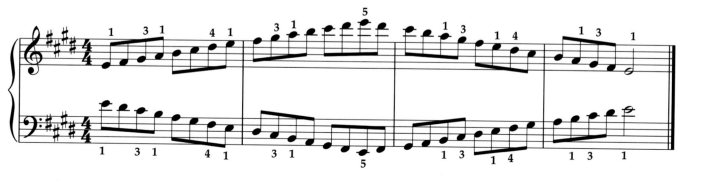

PRIMROSE
AN E MAJOR SCALE STUDY

PRIMROSE
AN E MAJOR SCALE STUDY

Let's put some pop in your triad training with lead sheets. **A lead sheet** uses chord symbols above the treble staff in place of the bass staff. Chord symbols dictate which chords your left hand plays while accompanying your right hand.

LET'S GET STARTED

1 The E major triad consists of the I chord (root) and its first and second inversions. Let's practice playing the triad of E major. We'll begin with a solid triad.

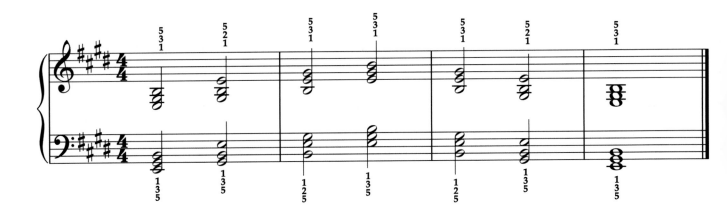

▶ Now let's practice playing the broken triad of E major. When playing a broken triad your tone should be smooth and even. Be careful not to accent the first note of each broken inversion.

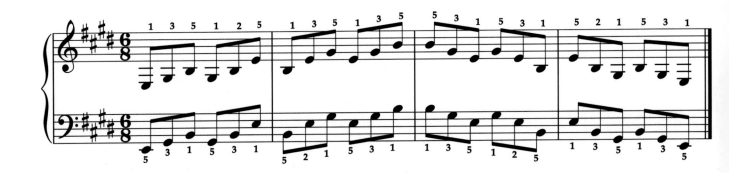

2 Next, let's learn how to play from a lead sheet. When playing from a lead sheet, the chord symbols are performed as held fifths, like this:

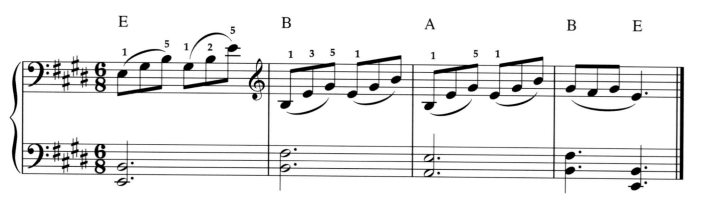

3 Finally, play the lead sheet below to rock the E major triad (add pedal when comfortable).

SIGHT READING

Let's explore the primary chords of E major. Can you find the I, IV, V, and vi chords in the music below?

Beginning at the red box and ending at the blue box, play the four measures of music that rest on the path. Next, I will use a colored crayon to draw a new four-measure path that begins at the red box and ends at the blue box. Try playing along the new path. Let's play again.

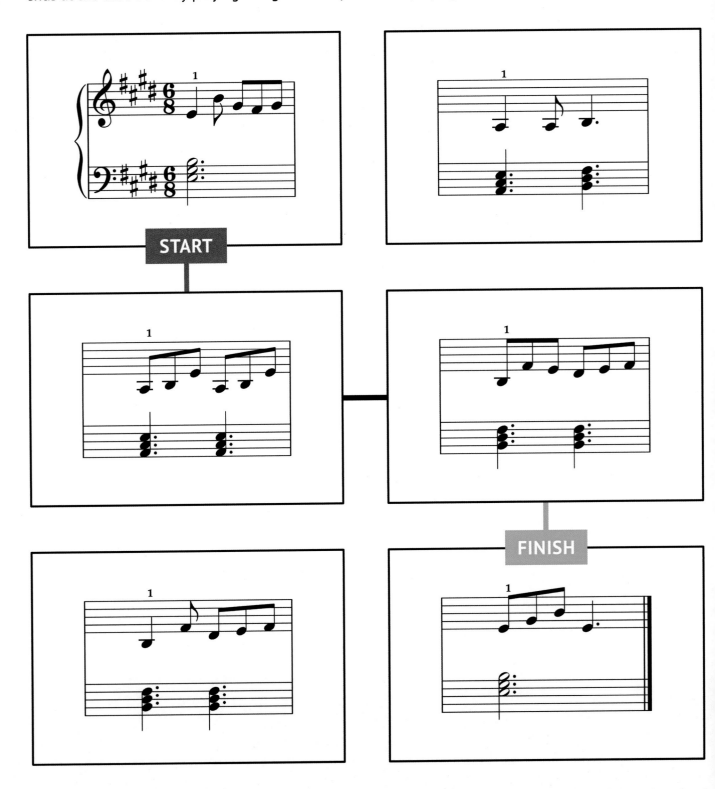

LAP TAP CLAP DUET

Let's reinforce the primary chords of E major with a Lap Tap Clap Rhythm Duet.

To begin, practice the body percussion above the grand staff below. Stem-down notes are performed by tapping both hands on your lap. Stem-up notes are performed by clapping your hands together. X note heads are performed by tapping your knuckles on a hard surface. Next, I will play the music as an accompaniment while you perform the body percussion. **Finally, let's switch roles.**

POP IMPROV
LEFT-HAND PATTERNS

Let's create a pop-worthy piano experience with left-hand patterns and improvisation. To begin, practice the left-hand pattern below. Then, when you are ready, show off your improv skills on the piece that follows this page.

LET'S GET STARTED

1 First, practice playing the broken chord pattern on the primary chords below.

E (I)   **A (IV)**   **B (V)**   **C#m (vi)**

2 Using any combination of notes from the E major five-finger scale, practice improvising a melody to match the provided rhythm as you play the left-hand chord progression below.

HOMETOWN
A POP PATTERN STUDY

Let's try again! As you play this piece, use any combination of notes from the
E major five-finger scale to improvise a melody that matches the provided rhythm.

C SHARP MINOR
C SHARP MINOR

It's time to power up your piano skills in the key of C sharp minor with pop-infused scale practice, lead sheet triad training, chord crunching, and left-hand pattern improv. **Let's get started!**

C SHARP MINOR MAP

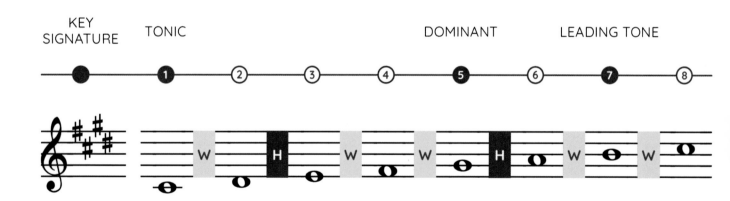

| KEY SIGNATURE | TONIC | | | | DOMINANT | | LEADING TONE | |

POP PIANO CHORDS

i	iv	v	VI
C# MINOR	F# MINOR	G# MINOR	A MAJOR

C SHARP MINOR SCALE PRACTICE

NATURAL MINOR SCALE

Practice playing a two-octave C sharp natural minor scale using the fingering patterns on the keyboard images and the notes on the grand staff.

LH Pattern

RH Pattern

HARMONIC MINOR SCALE

When playing the C sharp harmonic minor scale, the leading tone (7th) is raised a half step. This is indicated by the colored notes on the staff below. Practice playing the scale.

LIGHTHOUSE
A C SHARP MINOR SCALE STUDY

With Expression

LIGHTHOUSE
A C SHARP MINOR SCALE STUDY

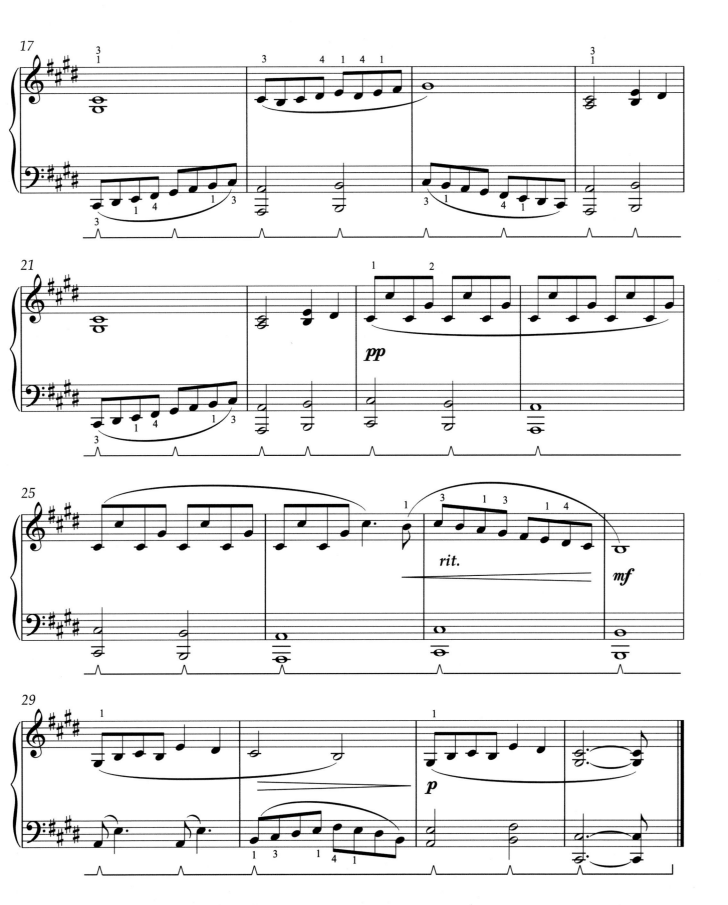

C SHARP MINOR
C SHARP MINOR

Let's put some pop in your triad training with lead sheets. **A lead sheet** uses chord symbols above the treble staff in place of the bass staff. Chord symbols dictate which chords your left hand plays while accompanying your right hand.

LET'S GET STARTED

1 The C sharp minor triad consists of the i chord (root) and its first and second inversions. Let's practice playing the triad of C sharp minor. We'll begin with a solid triad.

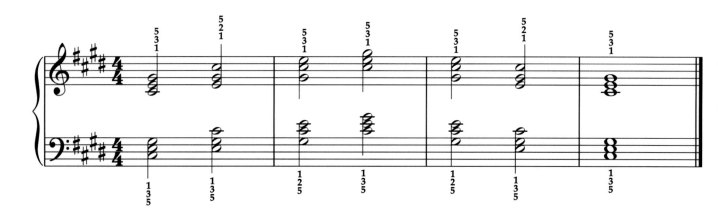

▶ Now let's practice playing the broken triad of C sharp minor. When playing a broken triad your tone should be smooth and even. Be careful not to accent the first note of each broken inversion.

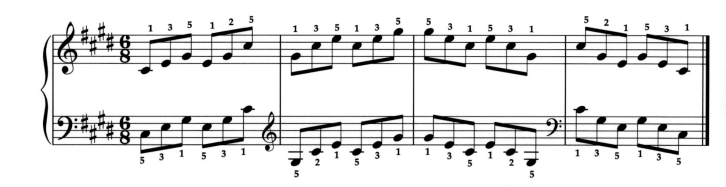

2 Next, let's learn how to play from a lead sheet. When playing from a lead sheet, the chord symbols are performed as held fifths, like this:

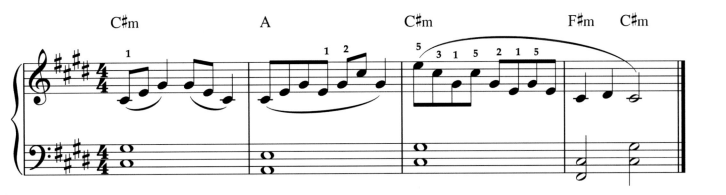

3 Finally, play the lead sheet below to rock the C sharp minor triad (add pedal when comfortable).

SIGHT READING

Let's explore the primary chords of C sharp minor. Can you find the i, iv, v, and VI chords below?

Beginning at the yellow box and ending at the purple box, play the four measures of music that rest on the path. Next, I will use a colored crayon to draw a new four-measure path that begins at the yellow box and ends at the purple box. Try playing along the new path. Let's play again.

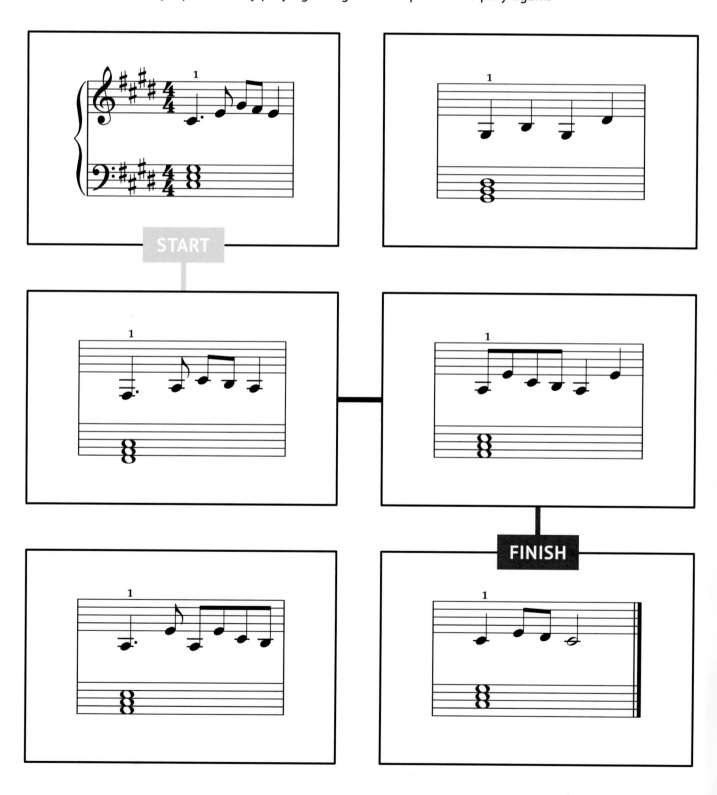

LAP TAP CLAP DUET

Let's reinforce the primary chords of C sharp minor with a Lap Tap Clap Rhythm Duet.

To begin, practice the body percussion above the grand staff below. Stem-down notes are performed by tapping both hands on your lap. Stem-up notes are performed by clapping your hands together. X note heads are performed by tapping your knuckles on a hard surface. Next, I will play the music as an accompaniment while you perform the body percussion. **Finally, let's switch roles.**

POP IMPROV
LEFT-HAND PATTERNS

Let's create a pop-worthy piano experience with left-hand patterns and improvisation. To begin, practice the left-hand pattern below. Then, when you are ready, show off your improv skills on the piece that follows this page.

LET'S GET STARTED

1 First, practice playing the syncopated polka pattern on the primary chords below.

C#m (i)   **F#m (iv)**   **G# (V)** *raised 7th   **A (VI)**

2 Using any combination of notes from the treble C sharp minor five-finger scale, practice improvising a melody to match the provided rhythm as you play the left-hand chord progression.

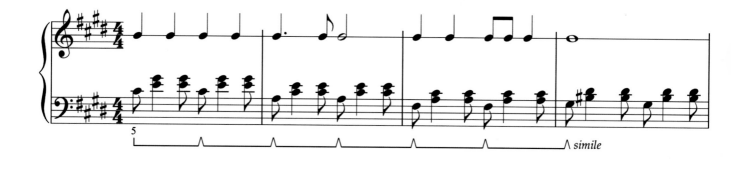

FALLING
A POP PATTERN STUDY

Let's try again! As you play this piece, use any combination of notes from the treble
C sharp minor five-finger scale to improvise a melody that matches the provided rhythm.

A FLAT MAJOR
A FLAT MAJOR

It's time to power up your piano skills in the key of A flat major with pop-infused scale practice, lead sheet triad training, chord crunching, and left-hand pattern improv. **Let's get started!**

A FLAT MAJOR MAP

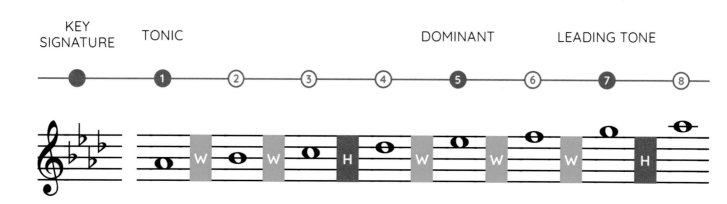

KEY SIGNATURE	TONIC				DOMINANT		LEADING TONE	

POP PIANO CHORDS

I	IV	V	vi
A♭ MAJOR	D♭ MAJOR	E♭ MAJOR	F MINOR

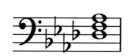

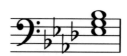

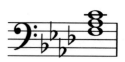

A FLAT MAJOR SCALE PRACTICE

A FLAT MAJOR SCALE

Practice playing a two-octave A flat major scale using the fingering patterns on the keyboard images and the notes on the grand staff.

LH Pattern

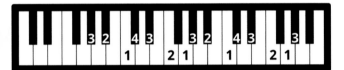

RH Pattern

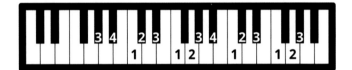

CONTRARY MOTION

Practice playing a two-octave A flat major scale in contrary motion. When you are ready, play the scale-focused pop piano piece on the following page.

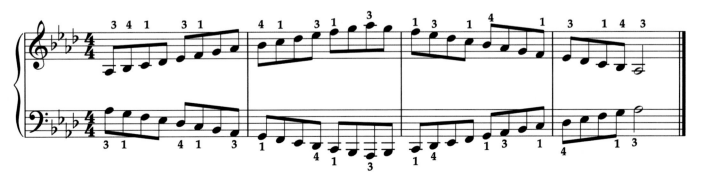

PARADISE
AN A FLAT MAJOR SCALE STUDY

PARADISE
AN A FLAT MAJOR SCALE STUDY

A FLAT MAJOR
A FLAT MAJOR

Let's put some pop in your triad training with lead sheets. **A lead sheet** uses chord symbols above the treble staff in place of the bass staff. Chord symbols dictate which chords your left hand plays while accompanying your right hand.

LET'S GET STARTED

1 The A flat major triad consists of the I chord (root) and its first and second inversions. Let's practice playing the triad of A flat major. We'll begin with a solid triad.

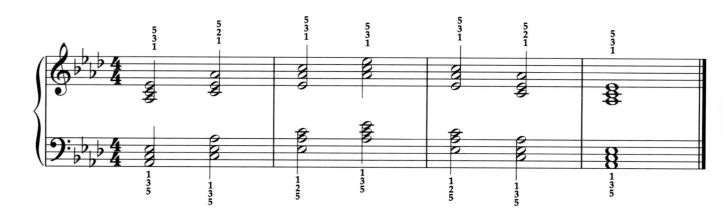

▶ Now let's practice playing the broken triad of A flat major. When playing a broken triad your tone should be smooth and even. Be careful not to accent the first note of each broken inversion.

2 Next, let's learn how to play from a lead sheet. When playing from a lead sheet, the chord symbols are performed as held fifths, like this:

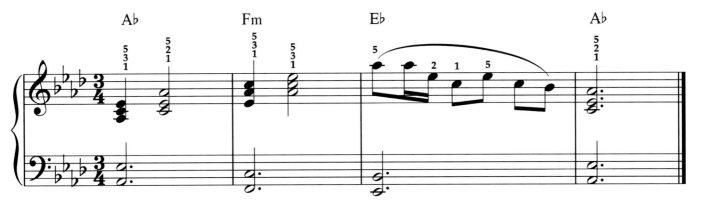

3 Finally, play the lead sheet below to rock the A flat major triad (add pedal when comfortable).

SIGHT READING

Let's explore the primary chords of A flat major. Can you find the I, IV, V, and vi chords below?

Beginning at the blue box and ending at the red box, play the four measures of music that rest on the path. Next, I will use a colored crayon to draw a new four-measure path that begins at the blue box and ends at the red box. Try playing along the new path. Let's play again.

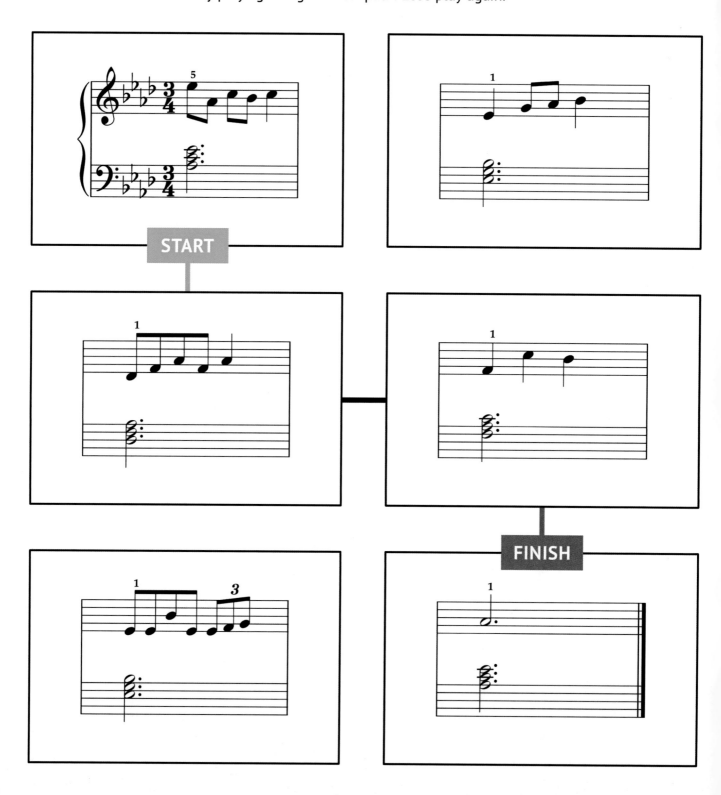

LAP TAP CLAP DUET

Let's reinforce the primary chords of A flat major with a Lap Tap Clap Rhythm Duet.

To begin, practice the body percussion above the grand staff below. Stem-down notes are performed by tapping both hands on your lap. Stem-up notes are performed by clapping your hands together. X note heads are performed by tapping your knuckles on a hard surface. Next, I will play the music as an accompaniment while you perform the body percussion. **Finally, let's switch roles.**

POP IMPROV
LEFT-HAND PATTERNS

Let's create a pop-worthy piano experience with left-hand patterns and improvisation. To begin, practice the left-hand pattern below. Then, when you are ready, show off your improv skills on the piece that follows this page.

LET'S GET STARTED

1 First, practice playing the crossover pattern on the primary chords below.

A♭ (I)　　　**D♭ (IV)**　　　**E♭ (V)**　　　**Fm (vi)**

2 Using any combination of notes from the A flat major five-finger scale, practice improvising a melody to match the provided rhythm as you play the left-hand chord progression below.

simile

PROMISES
A POP PATTERN STUDY

Let's try again! As you play this piece, use any combination of notes from the
A flat major five-finger scale to improvise a melody that matches the provided rhythm.

Gracefully

F MINOR
F MINOR

It's time to power up your piano skills in the key of F minor with pop-infused scale practice, lead sheet triad training, chord crunching, and left-hand pattern improv. **Let's get started!**

F MINOR MAP

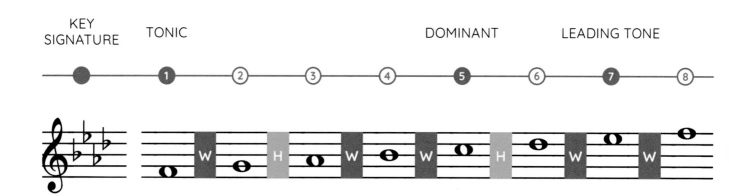

| KEY SIGNATURE | TONIC | | | | DOMINANT | | LEADING TONE | |

POP PIANO CHORDS

i	iv	v	VI
F MINOR	B♭ MINOR	C MINOR	D♭ MAJOR

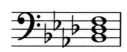
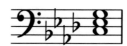

F MINOR
SCALE PRACTICE

NATURAL MINOR SCALE

Practice playing a two-octave F natural minor scale using the fingering patterns on the keyboard images and the notes on the grand staff.

LH Pattern

RH Pattern

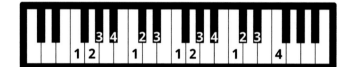

HARMONIC MINOR SCALE

When playing the F harmonic minor scale, the leading tone (7th) is raised a half step. This is indicated by the colored notes on the staff below. Practice playing the scale.

VOYAGER
AN F MINOR SCALE STUDY

With Fervor

VOYAGER
AN F MINOR SCALE STUDY

Let's put some pop in your triad training with lead sheets. **A lead sheet** uses chord symbols above the treble staff in place of the bass staff. Chord symbols dictate which chords your left hand plays while accompanying your right hand.

LET'S GET STARTED

1 The F minor triad consists of the i chord (root) and its first and second inversions. Let's practice playing the triad of F minor. We'll begin with a solid triad.

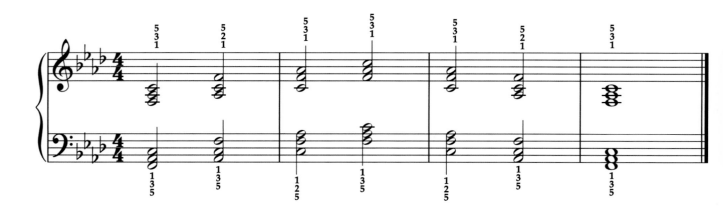

▶ Now let's practice playing the broken triad of F minor. When playing a broken triad your tone should be smooth and even. Be careful not to accent the first note of each broken inversion.

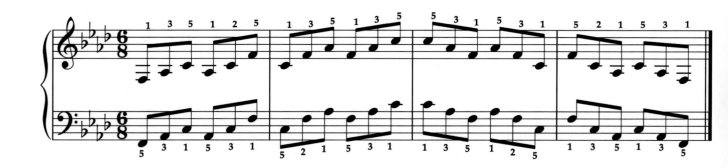

2 Next, let's learn how to play from a lead sheet. When playing from a lead sheet, the chord symbols are performed as held fifths, like this:

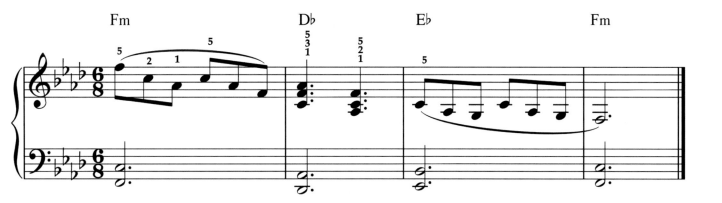

3 Finally, play the lead sheet below to rock the F minor triad (add pedal when comfortable).

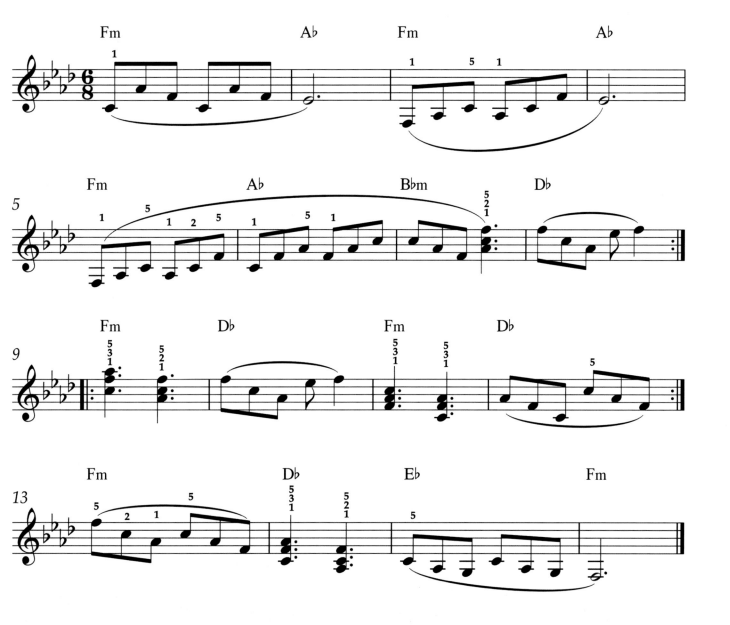

SIGHT READING

Let's explore the primary chords of F minor. Can you find the i, iv, v, and VI chords in the music below?

Beginning at the red box and ending at the green box, play the four measures of music that rest on the path. Next, I will use a colored crayon to draw a new four-measure path that begins at the red box and ends at the green box. Try playing along the new path. Let's play again.

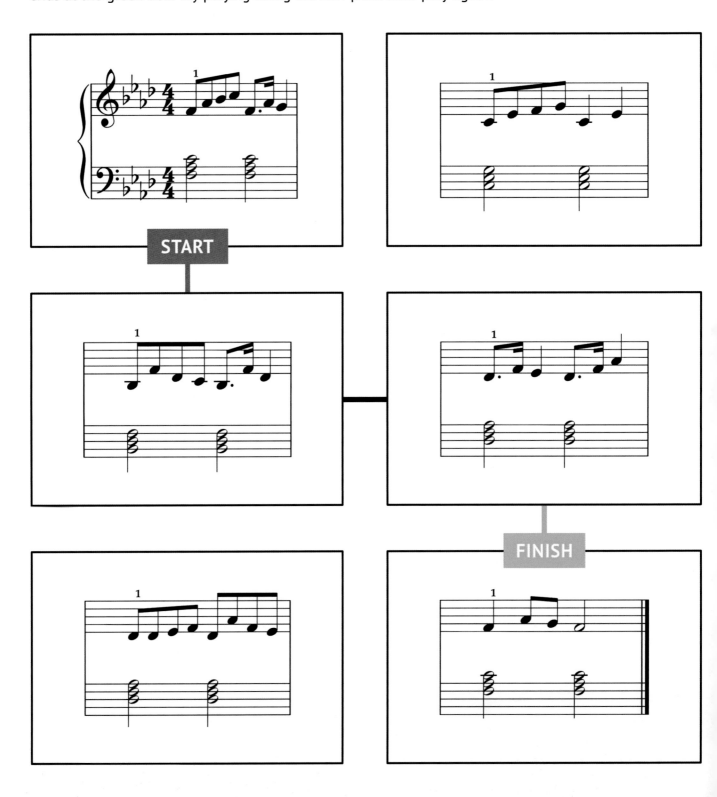

LAP TAP CLAP DUET

Let's reinforce the primary chords of F minor with a Lap Tap Clap Rhythm Duet.

To begin, practice the body percussion above the grand staff below. Stem-down notes are performed by tapping both hands on your lap. Stem-up notes are performed by clapping your hands together. X note heads are performed by tapping your knuckles on a hard surface. Next, I will play the music as an accompaniment while you perform the body percussion. **Finally, let's switch roles.**

POP IMPROV
LEFT-HAND PATTERNS

Let's create a pop-worthy piano experience with left-hand patterns and improvisation. To begin, practice the left-hand pattern below. Then, when you are ready, show off your improv skills on the piece that follows this page.

LET'S GET STARTED

1 First, practice playing the alberti bass pattern on the primary chords below.

Fm (i)   **B♭m (iv)**   **C (V)** *raised 7th   **D♭ (VI)**

2 Using any combination of notes from the F minor five-finger scale, practice improvising a melody to match the provided rhythm as you play the left-hand chord progression below.

MIDNIGHT
A POP PATTERN STUDY

Let's try again! As you play this piece, use any combination of notes from the
F minor five-finger scale to improvise a melody that matches the provided rhythm.

Steadily

Made in the USA
Las Vegas, NV
24 August 2024